MW01105643

TAKING THE BREATH AWAY

OTHER BOOKS BY HAROLD RHENISCH

Poetry

Winter (1981)
Eleusis (1986)
A Delicate Fire (1989)
Dancing with My Daughter (1993)
Iodine (1994)

Non-Fiction

Out of the Interior: The Lost Country (1993)

Taking
the Breath
Away

—

by
Harold Rhenisch

RONSDALE PRESS

1998

RONSDALE PRESS
3350 West 21st Avenue
Vancouver, B.C. Canada
V6S 1G7

Set in New Baskerville 11 on 14
Typesetting: Julie Cochrane, Vancouver, BC
Printing: Hignell Printing, Winnipeg, Manitoba
Cover Design: Ewa Pluciennik

Ronsdale Press wishes to thank the Canada Council for the Arts, the Department of Heritage, and the British Columbia Cultural Services Branch for their support of its publishing program.

CANADIAN CATALOGUING IN PUBLICATION DATA
Rhenisch, Harold, 1958–
   Taking the breath away

   Poems.
   ISBN 0-921870-55-8

   I. Title.
PS8585.H54T34 1998   C811'.54   C97-911040-8
PR9199.3.H464T34 1998

for

EBERHARD

ACKNOWLEDGEMENTS

The author thanks the editors of the following magazines
where some of the poems in this book were first published:

"The Fish" in *Arc*

"Trees" and "The Brothers" in *Canadian Literature*

"Charlie Manson Comes to Town" in *The Fiddlehead*

"Running Horses" and "Taking the Breath Away"
in *The Malahat Review*

CONTENTS

A FIELD GUIDE TO ANGELS

Taking the Breath Away   11
A Field Guide to Angels   13
Moving a Greenhouse   14
The Lake   16
Trees   17
The Secret of Photosynthesis   19
Guide to Canadian Architecture   21
A Layman's Guide to Literary Criticism   23
Running Horses   24
Sharing the Mouth of the Wind among Friends
and Consecrants   26
Dead Heads   28
Agamemnon, 1990, Keremeos   31
A Guide to Euclidian Geometry   33
Reading Eliot With One Hand Tied
Behind Your Back   35
Preface to the Canadian Edition of
Plato's *Republic*   37

THE LAKE IS BOTTOMLESS

At the Beginning of the World   41
The City Without Angels   43
Summer Wind   45
The King in the Snow   46
The Black Birds   47
The Bishops   49
The Sound of Birth   50

Sunflowers   51

The Dog   53

The City of Witches   54

Swallows   56

The Song of the Whales   58

The Sun is Everything   59

THE MISSING WATER

The Trick for Reading Rilke   63

The Brothers   64

A Private Screening   66

Neah Bay   70

Charlie Manson Comes to Town   72

The Woman With the Violin   74

The German Eagle   76

The Wasp Nest   78

Seeing Colours in a Black and White World   80

The Fish   82

What to Do When You Look Out and
Robert Graves is Standing Outside Your Window
Twisting His Hands   83

Horses   85

Spring Poem for Betsy and Lawrie   87

The Night Lake   92

About the Author   95

—

A FIELD GUIDE
TO ANGELS

—

Taking the Breath Away

In the high plateau
the thistles grow taller than a horse,
with spines an inch long.

They have brilliant purple flowers
and for seeds the down of birds.

Among them men plant cabbages and beets.

There is a kind of paint
which is the colour of a woman's lips,
of the thin sap of a thistle,
of a horse as it stands out in the rain.

As brilliant green beetles
fly out of the reedbeds
and into the pine forests,
the thistles dream of the sea,
where the fish say one word
a thousand times each hour
and never twice the same.

An old grey horse
stands shoulder-deep in thistles,
with bird down in his mane,

and stares at the horse
that stares at him
out of the black glass
of an empty shed.

Sometimes he stands there
for an entire day,

until a woman comes
in a blue coat
with a handful of oats in her hand
and leads him away.

As they walk through the pasture together
the horse nuzzles her pocket.

The stars shine suddenly
alone in the empty sky.
It takes the breath away,
a thousand times

and never the same twice.

A Field Guide to Angels

In a field guide to birds
you won't find angels,
with their white dresses
and their dark nipples
and their voices of walnut wood.

Sometimes I have heard women
who were violins. They spoke
with the voices of strings they stroked
with their fingertips, setting my bones
trembling, so that for a moment
I was the music that played them.

I have watched small birds
eat white berries in first snow.
There was an angel among them
in the bushes: a breath of cold,
a green evening light,
the rose-coloured bark of the trees.

Now I am writing a field guide to angels.
It's music I need.

Moving a Greenhouse

The first weather sign for Rain: Barn.

The other signs: Glass;
Wing;
Shattered seed; sun all day,
with brief showers toward evening,
mauve light through the willows,
a flower spilling out dusk;
a broken flask;

high wind, tattered cirrus.

The weather sign for ash: black knife
of the tongue,

broken jar of the night.

Those signs are the eyes.
Those are the windows.
Those are the laughter
in the fingers
that dance over the Earth's skin,
like a drum
made of petals,
a breath made of bees,
a splinter of the evening breeze
brought across such a distance
it is now a word.

They have placed it under glass.
The people crowd around,
behind ropes.

Art used to be to honour the dead,
by aiding them to cross the river
without memory. *That*
was the hard part of life, to keep it going
without the body,
and, above: the sky,
absolutely clear,
absolutely empty.

This is the weather sign for night:
clouds on the horizon,
men raking the loose soil
under the blighted fruit trees
of their heat-parched gardens,

taking the air in by great mouthfuls,

and within them slow, giant fish —
moving behind their eyes,
pushing their flanks
up against the glass
as they slide by —

breathing, slowly,
under the carbon dioxide skies.

The Lake

If I had to be a house
I would be a window —
it breaks.

If I had to be a floor
I would be the tiles —
they chill the feet,
and the body remembers the earth.

But if I had to be a room in a house,

I pray I would be the bedroom.
The bedroom
is awake all night in a cold sweat,

chest-deep with the lake of dreams.

Slow, black fish
slip in and out of the shadows.

It is deepest night.
A skim of ice
forms on the surface of the water.

The stars blow overhead.
Black wind.

A lone teal
rises off the water
into the silence.

Trees

Trees dream they will be horses some day.
They stand in the blue rain and gently shake their hair.

Sometimes they laugh for a whole year, then they sleep
until the horizon startles up and stares into the black mouth
between the stars.

When the chickens settle on their branches at dusk,
only the saplings giggle; the older trees hold their breath,
for they know that God
made chickens because he missed his angels.
Trees know about love.

In the mountains the trees call for the sea.
In the night the waves crash and crash on the shore.

While the cows sleep under their branches
with their eyes open, the trees listen to the chiselling
of the violin maker in a mountain town. They remember
God very well, even though he only spoke to them once;
he was everything that you couldn't see,
everything which now streams with light.

Sometimes they ride the moon as if it were a horse.
Sometimes the moon crawls into their branches.
Then they embrace her and sing.

In the winter, trees go around naked,
so that in the moonlight their beautiful bodies
will be transformed into silver.

When the fire comes, they are smoke.
When war comes, they follow the soldiers
on the tips of their toes, with a finger on their lips.
In the night they fly quietly through the air,
dragging their roots behind them
like jellyfish in the sea.

They remember the first day of the world,
when the fish were swimming in the dark ground.
The trees walked through the fields,
caught the fish, and washed them with water.
Because of that the fish can't remember the earth at all,
and the trees know that nothing is new
and everything will be renewed.

The Secret of Photosynthesis

Hands-on display:

scythe,
stone,
water.

The water is not for the stone.
It is for you.

The stone is to be used dry.
You will smell it shredding on the blade.

Just as the water
is drawn up into the tree
by the evaporation of water

— a lazy man's guide to breathing —

or the mallow
that ripens its seeds
even when yanked out of the soil,
even when it's withered,

you leave out what must
be included, by definition,

you *include* a frame for light.

What you cannot see
is what you can see.

What you expect
is what you should put into an envelope
and send off,

with no return address.

Return every night to your first home.

Guide to Canadian Architecture

Just what the hell is a nature poem . . . ?
          —Robert Kroetsch

The walls here hold up the roof,
which holds up the sky.

To understand the necessary physics:
drink a tree right out of your hands,
whisper a spider with your heels.

Not all houses can be beautiful,
because not all men

have suffered Robert Kroetsch & Co., Movers,

to deconstruct their house,

but there! there! it's gonna be alright,

the stars will appear
through the mosquito light
and the wind will suck at the grass stems
with its teeth.

I promise.

Look, when the government
pushed down Hans Feldt's
orchard house in Naramata,

after having relocated him
to the Haven Hill Retirement Centre in Penticton,

the house exploded in a cloud of bats
when the Cat touched the first wall,

right in front of the waiting trucks.

But he came back. A ghost, sure,
yet he lived with me for the whole summer

as I thinned apricots,
flicking them between my fingers
into the grass, on those white
cliffs above the lake,

giving me the sky,
as a gift,

and the earth as a chain.

I'd read Virgil, outside,
under the pear trees,

until the light was so thin
the words were only the sound of the wind
in the stiff leaves,

and the bull snake
slipped through the grass —

a fire that gave off no light.

When you build a house,
build it by hand,

with some idea of the people
who will live there

with all their children.

A Layman's Guide to Literary Criticism

There are some prerequisite tools:
musk-oxen circled against the wind,
sparse grass,
rock.

Against a summer sky as blue as ice
we stand like cairns of stones
pointing the way
to winter.

Literary criticism is not about literature
after all, but about a choice of tools:

a Black & Decker variable speed reversing
rechargeable drill

or a brace and bit.
They both make holes.

Poetry: a barn full to the roof with hay,
and rats running around, squealing;

words for winter;
translations for snow
that drifts across the yard,

out of the air on one side,
into the air on the other,

and Van Gogh
in his last weeks
standing out there,
watching us fall.

Running Horses

The window is a hand. It is on fire.

A hundred men
have gathered in the work yard today
for an auction of tractors
and hay rakes.

They balance on the pole fences.
Their eyes smell of diesel.

Around their feet dandelions spray out
like small natural gas wells.

The jack pines are brown and dirty.
It is spring.
The cattle eat the new
grass among the aspen stumps.
It is on fire.

Men ride horses as if they were birds made
out of turquoise and wind.
The hands of the men smell like the moon.

They have amber broken nails.

They raise their hands
and point out rotovators
and spring-tooth harrows,

but the wind tears away their words

and no one knows what it is
that they say.

The next day the yard is empty.
No one has put the wild fires out.
The cattle nuzzle them with their noses
but do not eat them.

When they move on
their noses are yellow:
the sun in a sky of water.

The bark of the rail fences
is dry and brittle
to the fingertips. Small lichens
cover each flake of bark:
pale green, grey, white.

The horses stomp through the sky.
Only their feet touch the earth.
They are insulated by thick hooves of bone.
The horses are lightning.

When you ride them
you must hang on tight.

Sharing the Mouth of the Wind
Among Friends and Consecrants

Full moon last night.

The sky a wind looked at on edge.

Damsel flies sitting on the thistles —
the field shimmering, blue,
then lifting off, scattered.

Words set out along a fence rail,
kid with a .22 — the old need to extend the mind
into the territory of the body.

Without patience, without sorrow,
the edges are wearing off each molecule of water.

World like molten glass,
whole sky like a lung.

The moon dreams me.

The trees tip-toe around us, and flee:
ghosts of insatience.

We lie in the grass side by side,
cold, drenched with dew.

Words like the edge of a file
slid across a knuckle,

like the hundred knives of a saw blade
cutting through the jeans into the knee.

Patience an old myth
gathered from a distant tribe,
and celebrated in the biggest cities.

Rain.

Dead Heads

for Ray Eno

The crows are returning
from a concert of the Grateful Dead.
They are dressed in rags, and flap
and flatter above the firs
and lodgepole pines
on the ridge above a shallow green lake.

The crows are stoned.
Some fly south, some west,
but after five minutes they are back
and fall into the trees,
laughing.
They have been smoking bulrushes.

The sun is a pool of pollen
floating on the water.
The grebes dive into it
and come up yellow,
with silver fish
in their long beaks.

The crows
clutch the scaly grey branches tightly
and roar.
Those that don't hold on
tightly enough
fall down
amid the branches
and stand
under the trees
in the tall yellow grass, dazed.

The crows like the drummer the best.
They pick up sticks
and try to beat out the rhythm —
as they remember it.
The sticks fall down
through the branches
and smash
the other crows on the heads.
They hop aside
lightly. They are doing the twist.

The sun reforms
and the grebe dives again,
the sun rippling behind him.

Some of the crows dream
of getting graduate degrees
in psychology. In an age of doubt
they are trying to invent electricity.
They stomp through the tall grass.
They smoke the black-seeded sedges.
That is their first step.
So far they are still trying to perfect it.

They understand everything.
They know the words of every song by heart.
It's not a lot of songs really,
but then their hearts aren't very big —
and neither is the sun.
It covers acres of the lake
but it is very very thin.
You can slip inside it
and make paintbrushes of your hands.
You can turn yourself into grass
and lose the wind.
You can store it inside a stone

and drop it into the sun
and through the sun
and while you hold your breath
watch the sun
explode.

Agamemnon, 1990, Keremeos

I saw the sun
bury its thorax in the earth
and lay its eggs.

I saw the moon
clamber over the mountains
on its web, its front legs waving,
feeling its way.

And I saw fire
in the sap of a milkweed.

I tasted the river
in a stone.

There is enough venom
in a cup of dust
to kill a man.

You don't have to look far.

There is enough care
in an aphid
to knock a star
out of that old tin sphere
above us,

the way you knock an apricot off a branch
with a rubber hose and a stick

when you're thinning the crop.

The words that come upon us
sometimes step right over us,
as if we weren't even there on the road,

between dreams

that flit across the brainpan
like water striders across a pond.

The water that you drink
was once a god

and has the fire
necessary to kindle us,

to burn us away —
a book of matches

struck all at once.
And then smoke, drizzling up
from each paper thumb.

A Guide to Euclidian Geometry

First the axiom:

the hand can speak,
the foot can breathe,

and the bones can hang
in a burlap sack from a tree branch
and invent philosophies,
mathematics,
poetry,
and God.

Then the second axiom:

when the landscape is invested
with the thoughts of the body,

the mind is free.

White dress. Backlit. Dancing in the daisies.
Golden hair.

Now the theorem, the axioms pushed together in a cookie tin,
and the lid jammed on:

the poles of experience are space
and the destruction of space,

time, and the destruction of time,
as we shake ourselves free from the land

with an old wooden flail
on the packed clay of the farmyard,

in rage at ourselves
for having shot our God in the chest

while out hunting pheasants,
the gun cocked under the arm

and then suddenly lifted, bang!
almost without looking. And bang again!

Proof:

The pheasant calls from the high grass
of the abandoned farmyards every morning,

like the rusted hinge of a screen door
as a twelve-year-old girl bangs outside

to feed the chickens.

Reading Eliot with One Hand
Tied Behind Your Back

Well, first off, you have to leave *him*
out of it —

a man who struggles to erase himself
can in the end expect that,

if nothing else. And time,
fertilized by time's absence?

Now that's always struck me
as the oddest thing.

"Dry the pool, dry concrete."
We all whisper that in our sleep,

yet when I think of that pool,
it is full of water, cool, and blue.

Maybe it's because of the roses,
unpruned, overgrown, at the edges,

mounds of brown-edged petals
catching in the wind and drifting over the flagstones.

But the pool is full. Clear. Full of the sky
which is not sky, the voice which is not voice,

the memory which is a false memory,
the water that gloves the skin

like an embrace. Still, would you dare
dive into that pool? Not me.

You dive into the pool:
it's suddenly a rose.

You touch the rose:
there's nothing there,

just a grey city, grey light,
grey men,

and Tom wandering around, distracted,
saying:

Is that just me,
or is it you too?

Preface to the Canadian Edition of Plato's *Republic*

This book is bound with an iron clasp.

It has hands of wood.

It has no face.

Once you portage the first word,
remember:

what you remember
is what you have lost from your life;

what you forget
has hands of water.

When the wind drinks
your breath out of the leaves
you sing to

and all the other words
are coming in from the fields,
each one carrying a heavy stone,

what you forget
is a wall.

—

THE LAKE
IS BOTTOMLESS

—

At the Beginning of the World

An old soldier carries a yellow rooster
on his shoulder and eats a green apple
with a knife.

A fish lies on a table
and lets itself be photographed in the nude.

A young woman has dressed herself in water.
Her voice is as bright as rain.

The deer sit on boulders,
fold their left legs over their knees
and smoke cigars, while they discuss
the significance of Becoming
into the middle of the night.

The hands of simple people burn like matches.
Every man has a small lead case,
in which he keeps a mouthful of snow.

The cranes discover mathematics. They calculate
everything together: "There is twice as much
in the world as there is in the world!" they announce

in public. Newspaper editors eat peaches
and write poems on cigarette papers. In the middle
of the night they smoke them all philosophically.
Then it is the end. After that

the cats ate the lightning out of the clouds,
the trees carried the houses away on their backs,
the mountains shook off their glaciers, stood up,
and walked one by one into the sea.
Last to be seen were the crosses on their peaks,
floating in circles on the waves.

The fish flew colourfully through the air
while the cities burned. People travelled endlessly
in the desert. The sun
streamed out of the sky no longer but rose out of the soil,
where it had buried itself like a frog in the fall.
The earth was so bright that all people
believed they were blind;
the stars had settled down on the earth,
and the people could not tell if they had met another person
or a star, when they sensed a greeting
out of the darkness inside the light.

Then there was no more earth. Then our grandparents
had to emigrate to the darkness and build a new world there.
It was exhausting. All they had to work with
was what they had in their pockets:

a few coins, a brightly coloured pebble,
a couple of keys, a plug of tobacco, a golden watch,
and a few matches — the world in which we live,
waiting for the beginning of the world.

The City Without Angels

Freiburg im Breisgau

Long ago the angels lived in doorways.
Whenever people went in and out,
the angels had to step into the streets.
If it had snowed they were terribly cold:
all they had for shoes were sandals
woven out of reeds.

In that old city people had built shelters
for themselves and for their livestock;
they had built nothing for the holy birds.
Whenever it rained and the wind blew out of the west,
the angels sought refuge in the cathedral,

but the cathedral was built of stone: high, dark,
and cold. It held only a few low wooden pews,
without pillows, without blankets. The angels
would lay themselves out there head to head
and stare the whole night
thoughtfully at the dark stone sky.

On Sundays it was even worse:
the people streamed from the narrow alleys
into the cathedral. There was no room left
for the angels: they had to stand outside
in the square — in the hot sunlight, in the snow,
and in the black rain of the world.

In the nave the choir sang as beautifully as the boys
who sat on the knees of God and ate grapes out of his hands,
but in the square the angels watched the monsters
on the peak of the roof, listened to the hymns, and did not
sing a note, and said no word. They simply
waited until the people were finished.
They had blue faces. They were half frozen.
You see them now and think they are made out of stone.
They stand in gaps in the wall
and on the roof, solid, yet they are not made out of stone.
They are made from the song of the choir
and the red mouths of women.

They are waiting for us.
They know very well that they must wait
a long, long time. They have prepared themselves
for that. They have transformed themselves from ambassadors
into Waiting itself, while a black rain falls
in the night of the cities
and the doors in the empty gaps of the wall
are newly painted and tightly closed.

Summer Wind

Partenkirchen

The wind walks down the street
in heavy boots
leaving tracks of mud.
Around his neck a rabbit hangs,
that he shot upon the hill.
He throws it down beside the fountain
and drinks the black water
from the wooden basin
with his hands.
Children run into the street.
The wind walks through them like rain
for he knows the mountains
are goats: if he claps
they spring away
quickly and stop a hundred metres
off and graze.
Behind him the mud dries in the sun.
As the wind stands again on the meadow
he turns and claps.
The dust swirls briefly over the stones,
then vanishes among the houses,
where women sweep it
from around the feet of children
while they hum, and their white legs
flash beneath their skirts.

The King in the Snow

Linderhof

The king plays with a swan in the garden.
In the winter the farmers look up
from the valley and see the candles
burning in the snow. The king has dreams.
Wolves walk up from the forests on two legs,
and slip in through the mirrors
of the writing room. As each wolf leaps out
it is a thousand; as it lands
it is only one, standing there like a man.
A peacock struts through the snow
and screams. The king does not know his name.
He has never tasted water.
The sun rises over the blue snow
and a slow yellow wind blows in
through the trees; the air
in every room grows cold and every one
of the thousand candles
that have burnt all night dies.
The wicks smoke in thin threads.
Everywhere pools of snow
melt on the floors.
When the king walks into the bedroom
a peacock is lying in the middle of the bed
with a goldfish in its beak.
The king lies down beside it.
When he wakes again it is night
and a new world. He remembers nothing
of the day before: not that he is a goat;
not that he is a man; not that he is the snow
pooling on the floor. The king has dreams.
He is alone. He stares out his golden windows.

The Black Birds

Ringlikon

Black birds stand in the grain fields
and slowly and loudly scream.
They have voices of iron.
Their words are old rusted nails
that children find in a garden.

The sun burns in the wheat ears.
A toad lies in the cool soil
under a stone and stares
into the darkness of the earth.

There are days which you call the past
even before they rise out of the sea of the night.

In a week the men will come
to scythe the fields. Now
the legs and hips of the women
and the chests of the children walking through the grain
are wet and cold
in the fresh light,
while the birds leap from the towers of heaven
and fall like flickering ashes on the earth.

The toads breathe slowly
in and out.
It will soon be harvest.

The children cry out for joy in the thin air.
One day they will talk about the cold.
Shivering,
they will write down the iron voices
of the birds
in nights that smell of coal.

The Bishops

Salzburg

In the dark the bats fly
around the golden doves on the roof
of the cathedral. While a pale blue light
pours through the streets
the dead step out of their graves
in the soft stone of the cliff.
They pick up their old instruments,
but sitting out there in the sun
and the rain their violas
and harpsichords
have turned to dust. In the dark
the bishops on the roof
pace slowly in the moonlight
and stare down into the deep alleys
of the city. Young people
are dancing in the streets.
In the cathedral one candle is burning.
The bishops in their cloaks of gold
let it burn. They laugh
every time a bat flies through their golden hair.

The Sound of Birth

Hausberg

There is one town in the white mountains
where all the women have red hair.
They say the people there were foxes
when the world was made
of beech bark, the fluff of wild flower seeds
and dew, and that across the gorge
all the people were wild sheep
with long horns curled to the back
as they clattered over sharp stones.
No one knows for sure,
yet in the town of foxes
the houses are made of lime
and on the stone threshold of every house
lies a dog. People say
that one night in the spring
the trees walk down out of the mountains
into the streets, and rustle, dark and grey,
so thickly that no one can pass by or through.
No one knows when,
but there came a winter of heavy snow
after a summer of heavy rain
and in the spring the trees all bloomed
so brightly that the petals opened
with a soft sound, like a small stone
that falls through the air
from a high cliff, with no sound
of its falling anywhere.

Sunflowers

Herden

In the valley above the city of angels,
men who smoke cherrywood pipes
and dress in heavy wool clothes
grow sunflowers in fields so large
it takes a day to cross them.
The flowers tower overhead
and slowly turn their faces
to the sun. In the fall
the noise of the diesel tractors
splashes through their stalks.
Their seedheads are bent down to the black
and rain-swept soil. As the men bring the loads in,
the smoke curls up around their eyes,
and flocks of tiny brown birds
scatter.

It is said that the angels
have come for only a few years,
seeking cool water and to feel the clouds
rain on their faces, and that they have not
yet found a reason to leave. In every street
they have planted spreading green trees.
In the summer they sit in the shade
and drink tall glasses of beer
with lemon and laugh late at night,
but in the fall, when the golden leaves cling
trembling to the chairs and tables
and lie still around their feet,
the angels sit under the bare trees
over cups of hot coffee

as the sparrows gather in the branches
from all the high valleys and sing.

Then the birds leave suddenly
and as the clatter of the diesel tractors stills
on the wind the angels wait for the snow.

It comes first as a silence in the wind,
and then as the wind.

The Dog

The wind is black:
because he has eaten the crows,
because he swims at the bottom of the sea.

You dream you are fighting through deep snow.
You wake up exhausted, with the moon in your mouth.
It howls like the wind in the fir needles.

A thousand tiny insects
are taking the house apart piece by piece.

You stand in the middle of a forest.
The trees are flying away.
They are carrying the earth in their claws.

A dog stands in the middle of the desert
of space and howls.

The City of Witches

Freiburg im Breisgau

In the city of witches the starlight
catches in the narrow canals
that flow out of the forest into the lake;
if the tails of two cows become tangled,
pious young women give one
woman up to the men, who burn her
under the walls at noon;
in the hot sun the smoke pours up blackly,
and smoky flashes of fire and the woman's screams
float up over the steep roofs
into the white mouth of the sun.
Over the city of witches the sun is huge
and fills most of the sky.
After the burning, the women walk home
through the streets — at first a long column,
then breaking off house by house,
until each woman steps in alone
through her black door.

Late in the afternoon the sun burns
in the narrow channels of water
that flow through the city
from the forest into the reeds
twice the height of a man,
and burns on the face of the water.
The women have clay jugs
which they dip into the streams
of golden fire. When they lift the jugs
the water is black. Terrified,
and careful not to spill a drop,

they hurry back into their houses
without saying a word.

When the men built the cathedral
for their women, they threw the scrap stone
into the lake, cartload after cartload,
which they hauled down with heavy brown horses
breathing clouds in the cool morning.
The stone slipped into the water
without disturbing the surface
or raising the level of the water,
and the men know: the lake
is bottomless. They are quick with their work
and are careful not to slip in.
When one of them accidentally falls into the water
the others pull him out immediately,
by the hair if they have to,
for the men in the city of witches
do not know how to swim.

Swallows

Kuppenheim

The air is green in the evening.
Tiny brown fish swim in shallow water.
Leaves of light flicker over their backs.
Along the path to the castle
men and women walk between tall pear trees.
Out in those fields
women once grew hemp twelve feet high.
While their men were at war
they fed the stalks into noisy machines,
to separate the fibres from the leaves.
They sold the fibres in a city down the green river,
where slave workers from distant countries
wove them into heavy ropes to use on warships
when they came in from the grey fog,
but the leaves they fed to their cows,
for they had neither time nor land
to grow fodder.

To make cheese for their children,
every evening and every morning,
below the black mountains
where the moonlight burns like coal,
the women milked their tender-eyed cows
in barns of shadow where swallows nested
against the eaves
and sheltered from the rain.
Over the years the town grew famous for its cheese
and it sold for a high price in the tiny shops
in the deep alleys of the cities
down the river and was carried

on many grey steel ships
by men who would never walk
through the big wooden doors
into the still dark where the cows rustled
like the slow, lapping waves
of a shallow river under the women's hands,
as the swallows circled high in the green air,
tiny and black, in silhouette against tall clouds
hanging like a mountain range
of eternal snow.

But that was a long time ago.
Today the fields are planted by old women
with a few vegetables, berries and flowers
to cut and bring into their white houses
with the faded grey shutters, and in the evenings
as they look out through the flowered
white lace of their windows, the women see the swallows
soar high and alone above the fields
as the sun cuts in low and red above the horizon
and bursts through the tangled branches
of old pear trees.

The Song of the Whales

There is a country of white bears.

In that country the oceans are a deep violet
and the sun is a hand cut out of white cloth.

There is an eye in the centre of the sun.

There is another sun:
in the year when the men wandered far,
until the distant islands flicked their backs
and dipped down into the sea,
it sank into the cold black deeps.

It lies there now
with the bones of whales,
and slowly sways back and forth,
its lips pursed,
not uttering a sound.

All around it the whales pipe
and whistle and sing.
A thousand miles away
men put their ears
to the face of the water
and hear them call.

Deep underwater
the music carries
completely around the world.

The sun too is listening.

The Sun is Everything

In distant countries the sun is a bird
with a flaming green tail. Here
he is a man with a cloak of feathers
he has collected by dancing.
In his dance every moment
is the beginning of time.

In other countries the sun is a woman.
She combs her long hair.
She drinks from a mountain pool.

Some people say it is the same sun.
These people dress in leather and purple wool
dyed from flowers that grow on the edge of snow.

The people who herd cattle on the edges of cliffs
and eat cheese and drink apple wine
know the sun is not something you can see.
It is everything you cannot see in the world.

THE MISSING
WATER

The Trick for Reading Rilke

Patience.

These small, nocturnal mammals
characterized by shyness have

a preference for water, but
they have no heaviness in their bones

and leave only the faintest footprints,
even in damp silt. But

they will come out,
if you sit among them,

having first turned yourself into water.

The Brothers

The sun is a bluebird now
She sits in the arms of the birch

They talk all day about Lorne
who revived a piglet mouth to mouth

yesterday that was crushed by the sow
He has watched every one of his ewes

die in a breech birth His brother
fishes shrimp off Tofino

and Hornby Island sleeps in his boat
and has no other house on this earth

Yesterday the sun was an owl
She hid in the green veils of the night

She whispered to the roots of the aspens
that feather the air and they whispered back

about a woman with two fathers
who fish sheep on the Horse Lake Road

dragging their nets just inches off the sawdust
and who lift them together

There in the bottom of the net all crushed together
lie the pink and black piglets squirming

the sky is a sow her breath is hot her eyes are small
The fathers sort the piglets out and lay them in the straw

and cast the nets again But today
the sun is a mountain bluebird

she has slipped on her silk dress
Her skin smells of sweetgrass she stands

still with the birch at the shore all day
and sighs While under the ice the sheep mill about glowing

A Private Screening

The young man
with the earring
and the red hair

who travelled from England
to his mother's
magic house
under the oaks
in Victoria

to show his father
a film from Ireland
of Ben Bulben
and the blue streams
in which William Butler
Yeats fished
for salmon

and of the black
stone and ivy tower that
was his home
after he plotted revolution
with a green-eyed
red-haired woman
in a park
full of water lilies
and white swans

is dead too young
with only his mother
and his lover to hold
him and help him go

where we all
must soon

It is fitting
that the movie
ended with a walk
into a country
churchyard
with low walls of stone
set not to keep
anything or anyone
in or out
but to define simply
a space
to hold the charm
cast a cold eye
on life on death
horseman pass by
then the clear wind
over the brown
winter heather
and the clouds
streaming shredding
building in the sky

The sound
of the borrowed projector
did not matter
the chatter of conversation
with all the small
foot-high
goddesses on the mantel
behind the white and silver
screen
added only a richness
to the film

the accent of whose narrator
I could scarcely understand
but which held the youth
of the young man's father
when he travelled to Ireland
to drink porter and to beg
the dialect
from door to door

and so learn his craft
as a poet
in ancient
Ireland

It was the only time
I ever met the young
man with the single earring
and the flaming
red hair
although I love his mother
and his white-bearded
father well have eaten blood
sausage in the green
walled kitchen
have pruned
the apricot tree
growing over the glass
of the solarium
in the back of his mother's magic
and unpainted house
and feel blessed
to have been invited there
to share that
moment
together in Victoria
by the sea

The oaks flare
over the roof of the house
like a crown
and move all night
and are never still
They are very strong

Beneath them
and in their shade
the old King apples bloom
and swell
and grow on black
and purple limbs
covered with lichen
and pale green moss

while beside them
the house trembles
and shifts
and sighs

for the man and woman
who live within her
to whom she is home
and shelter

as are the trees
as is the light
as is the air

Neah Bay

The moon is a shell.
Behind it is another moon,
on fire: the phosphorescence of the sea.

The town we live in is so poor
the roofs have collapsed on all the motels.
The stink of the tide flats floats through the bush.

The men lie out among the alders
and stare into the hypnotic eye
of the beast of the sky.
They have no name to speak back.
They lie there all summer.

The women dress their children
in bright clothes and hold their hands
as they walk together
down the cracked lumps of asphalt
and concrete that line the road.

Used oil drums and fish boats
are rusting and rotting into the bay.
One child spends the entire afternoon
dragging a yard-long chunk of styrofoam
out of the cool blue throat of the sea
and over the highway — like a man with a whale
three hundred years ago.

But at night when the stars flit like birds
through the broad, flat leaves
of the alders the women come
to the men

and as the children sleep in the old
abandoned holiday trailers
and the six foot singlewides
abandoned by the loggers
among the mosquitoes,
together they speak with the birds

— and the birds answer them
with voices that are hot and husky,
and the leaves flutter
and flash and flare in the darkness —

as they lose themselves in each other

and step out again
into the cool and windy night.

Charlie Manson Comes to Town

We live in the town of ice,
deep underwater.
Charlie Manson is here
picking Siberian pears.
He came in a week ago,
his '69 Roadrunner
limping into the Petro–Can.

Every night the bears come
down from the hills to feed.
After a hot dry summer
there are no berries.
The bears carry rain and grass seeds
in their matted hair.
They too know
that the ice is coming.

Manson says he'll push north
as soon as he has enough pears
to pay for the repairs.
"Don't read books," he says.
"Don't tell people what you think."

He drinks a cup of mechanics' coffee
with a skim of 10W30 on the top
through a red plastic stir stick,
like a cappuccino at a drive-in espresso bar,
as the miles wind away in his eyes.
He has come a long way to be with us here.

He laughs,
cradling the paper cup in his hands
for the heat.

The nails are chewed off on his fingers.
"The sky is very black here," he says.
"It looks very old."

He sips the coffee again. His eyes
are riveting.
They are the eyes of a crow.
They are made of ice.

The leaves of the Uri pears
are tangled in his hair and beard.

As he sits
among the alternator belts
and the used studded tires,
a cloud slams up against the window
all at once,
like a rifle shot,

and the sun

rolls slowly over
and over down the centre line
of the highway. Behind it
a black wind
unrolls mile by mile,

as Manson stands and slowly
walks over and presses his face to the cool glass.

The Woman with the Violin

The young black-haired woman
with the red-hued
violin

lays a blue velvet cloth
on its hard body
and gently

rests her chin
against the cloth her
teeth clenched

For half an hour
she sits on the edge
of her yellow oak chair

throwing her whole
thin body
into the wood
through her shoulders and
through her chin

like a man
burying his face
into his lover's
light shoulder

as they sing
of yellow flowers
in the high
mountain grass

A red-tailed hawk
soars overhead
in the blue winds

while they fall
upward
and off the earth

like a woman
giving birth walking
out of her body
in mixed joy and pain

her body so far
below in a small
white room
her cries
and the cries of her child
unheard

yet becoming
through that bitter
effort a bird
carved and shaped
of thin
red wood

and through that bird
the song
the hard and bitter
alluring song
of love and birth
that forms
her

out of sound
and fire

The German Eagle

In Friesenhagen
Eberhard spread a map
of the two Germanys
on the wooden table

we bent low
under the fermented
hay-scent of old beams
our lips awash
in pale
French wine

as the moon
rose over the square
bell tower
behind us

I remember
the blue of a shirt

and a wisp
of grass and stars
washing up off the marshes
of the Northeast

as the paper crackled
under our fingers

Model and Dürer
standing over our shoulders
even their faces black
breathing
desperate

I remember white hands
fingernails cut short
and the ashen certainty
of war

Tonight the scent of steel
in the dark

and muffled voices
mocking us
from 1939

laughing right in our faces

I turn from the window
and begin again
to smell my fingers
grass fields
the sun flaring
like a wasp gone mad
with heat

a bird
in memory
flashing up
against the long rays
of a low sun
hunting

its shadow dissipating
in the amber air

And I cry out loud

(West Germany, 1987)

The Wasp Nest

There is a black wind
inside the trees: it is the night.

I've come to think lately:
what if she got out
through the snapped-off branches —
the mess a bear makes
in the choke cherries
in September?

Then what would happen
when the earth raised her shoulder
and drowned the sun?

The stars would cling to the branches
like drops of dew, and glisten.

Ants and birds
would move in
to the hollow trunks —

and the night would sit at our table,
with her wasp-nest head
and her birch-twig fingers,

her back to the window — tall,
creaking on the seat, uncomfortable, hot,

and silent —
for you could be certain
she would not speak.

You would have to have the strength
to speak the first words

of a new language.

Seeing Colours in a
Black and White World

A tall woman
with sharp cheekbones
and full red lips
who lives in a forest
outside a town of blue water
keeps sheep.

All winter she watches them
plow through the deep snow
for the meadow hay
her husband hauls.

Their breath rises above them
in small clouds
as does the breath of her husband
and that of her children
who build children out of snow
and come in again
with blue lips.

Late at night
as the wood burns
in the black iron stove
she makes kaleidoscopes
from crystal,
lead and coloured glass.

In the mornings
she shows them
to her children.

They hold them up
to the milk-white
light
that flakes against the window
and falls over the wooden floor,
and look in
and see the name of the sun.

When her husband comes in
from the snow for coffee,
meadow hay in his hair
and frost in his beard,
he lifts one up
and looks
and laughs
with the children,

while the sheep
mill about in the snow,
only their black
faces visible

in a white world.

The Fish

lie on the wall-to-wall carpet
while I listen to Bach.
They are small and yellow.
Trout swim slowly through the sunbeams
in the firs. The tuna are shadows.
They breathe our death in and our lives out.

Late at night I lie down in bed.
Instead of my wife, I find a salmon beside me.
She turns her head on the pillow and sorrowfully
watches me with the eyes of the sea.

In the spring, blue fish
swim in the face of the moon.
When the clouds drive in tatters,
the fish swim out into the purple sea.
They fall to the earth as rain.
They stream over my face.
I catch them with my hands.

They flow off the roof through the down pipe
and into the flower beds,

with the voices of birds,
that live under the earth
and have been calling us quietly

since the beginning of time.

What to do When You Look Out and Robert Graves is Standing Outside Your Window Twisting his Hands

Invite him in!

You might inquire about
your mutual friends:

> water,
> wood,
> wind,
> fire.

> Gold coins from the Queen.

He'll lead the conversation
around soon enough.

When he does:

> Cup your ear to your hand.

> Speak your mouth into the window.

> Clutch the house with your hair.

Let nothing out until he's done!

Someone's sharpening a scythe
on the other side of the thin door,

running his thumb

over the hot blade.

Give thanks if everything in the house
has been made by hand.

Everything will be released by its weight
from weight.

Horses

In their mouths, in their eyes, in their ears
the horses smuggle apples out of the orchards.
Horses know the dwarves who are taking the world apart.

Every horse is good friends with a film director.
In the afternoons horses let angels sit on their backs.
They carry them everywhere, with the precise footsteps
of ballet dancers. Horses are mathematicians.
They are calculating out love.

Once a white horse found a whale
stranded in a morning meadow.
He stood over her for the whole day
to shelter her from the sun, until it was night
once more and she could swim off into the black sea.

Every horse has a yellow bird
that sits in a nut tree on the edge of the field
and stares for the horse into the far distance.

Whenever bees crawl over their noses,
horses close their eyes tightly and recite Mallarmé.

Horses remember the first day of the world
and watch the last. They are not disappointed.
They run after butterflies.
They dream while they are awake.
They are awake the whole time that they sleep.
Horses count the stars: there's only one,
but they see it three thousand times!

Sometimes, many years ago, horses
stomped on top of submarines. They stood on the turrets
in order to see into the distance. Then the submarines
dove under the earth, and it was a long, long time
before the horses, looking for the way out, their footsteps
clanging on the iron subterranean pathways,
once again stepped into the waves of the wind.

When little girls bring them apples,
they kiss their hands.

They know no force.

Spring Poem for Betsy and Lawrie

The thin
and smiling woman
who is always
dancing

and who
leads her body
with her shoulders
and her up-turned
head
as if she is studying
at all times

while she opens a door
in an old
mahogany house
or walks
down the cracked
and up-lifted
concrete sidewalk
of a town
in a green
northern forest
under the whistling swans

the art of theatrical
improvisation

is sitting
at the mahogany
grand piano
tonight

on the white
stage of the church
of the Emissaries
of the Divine Light
to play
the story of Persephone

rising from the lightless
halls
of the master of lust
and bound earth

here in the last thin snow
of March
as the Hereford calves
lie on muddy
and trampled hay
with the sleet melting
on their rust
red coats
their heads burrowed
into their stomachs

The eagles
circle high overhead
at the turning and birth
of the year
out of the pale
green night skies
of winter cold

Right now the woman stands
and reaches in
to the strings of the piano
and strokes them broadly
as if each string

was a plait of hair
stretched out
to shape a breathing
harp

The sound is gentle
as the wind
in the first sticky
half-grown leaves
of the aspens
in the first
yellow days
of the year

Her friend
who is wearing
a green sackcloth gown
barefoot
suddenly lifts her head
and speaks

of a dark kingdom
in which there is no
king
only an oppressing
emptiness

and as suddenly
stops speaking

the woman
with the thin birdlike smile
sits again on the sharp-legged
bench of the piano
and peers forward
at the black notes

on the white paper

which she wrote there
in the winter
her brow furrowed and her fingers
following the smiling
blue movement
of her eyes

deciphering the notes just now
as she hears them
for the first time

again her friend speaks
to her and it is not
clear

to us
who have not
rehearsed
our listening

whether the words
of the woman
in the coarse gown
call the music
out of silence

or whether the music
plays her
like a cello

and she is an aspen
in the yellow spring
sun in the blue wind
suddenly given speech

then stilling
in the shadow of that speech
as the heat shines again
out of her white trunk

but it is clear
they are both
created from
our listening

these women
who are stepping
just now
as they always have
since the beginning
of given love
into sisterhood
and light
for the very
first time

and who have never
been so
strong
as they

are now

The Night Lake

At night the lake disappears
I walk down the mud slopes
while the fish rise
and fly through the air around me
blue and yellow and red
in swarms and flocks
the minnows like grasshoppers
the large fish like eagles and crows

There in the very deepest pools
I swim through the air
for a few hours
One by one the stars wink out
far overhead
as the light
begins to wash in blue
from the horizon

It settles around my feet
cool
and I know I must begin
again the long climb
out to the shore
where the reeds rustle
and the sopranos of the red dock
sing

And the fish know
they must slowly sink down
into the daytime pool
of their memory

When I climb out through the mud
I hear the fish behind me
one at a time
splash down
into the water

In the early morning
as I stand among the reeds
the green surface of the lake
stretches out before me
and the trout rise up to it
with their lips
and break
it

and every
touch of their mouths is
a drop of rain

ABOUT THE AUTHOR

Harold Rhenisch lives in the Cariboo country, the high vol-
canic plateau between the mighty Thompson and Fraser rivers
that drain the vast British Columbia Interior. Rhenisch's five
books of poetry explore the land on which he lives and where
he grew up in an immigrant culture developing orchards and
vineyards in the fertile Okanagan Valley. In the juxtaposition of
new European cultures and an ancient land, Rhenisch sees
again the Kenya of the 1920s portrayed by Karen Blixen in *Out
of Africa*. After waiting in vain for a V.S. Naipaul to write of the
colonial plantation cultures of the Okanagan, Rhenisch turned
his sense of the land into a vehicle capable of speaking for a
complex contemporary world: the autobiographical fiction of
Out of the Interior: The Lost Country.

For nearly twenty years, Rhenisch has striven to create an
authentic literature for the silent rural parts of Canada, to
place their images and dialects on an equal footing with those
of the modern urban world. At the same time, he has been a
student of Ezra Pound, post-modern German literature and
trickster mythology. His forthcoming prose work, *The New
World*, combines the immigrant's sense of displacement with
perennial images of life on the land. For Rhenisch, the twen-
tieth century — the century of war and slaughter — is over, and
the work of starting a new literature is paramount. *Taking the
Breath Away* reveals Rhenisch's passion for imagery and lyri-
cism, and shows that when these are centred in the workings of
consciousness and mythology the new vision can begin to
appear.